BRUCE GOLDSTONE

I SEE A PATTERN HERE

HENRY HOLT AND COMPANY

NEW YORK

Do You See a Pattern Here?

A pattern is something that repeats. It might repeat just once, or it might repeat again. And again and again. You get the idea. Some patterns can repeat forever. But in the real world, patterns usually stop repeating because they run out of room. You can spot many different kinds of patterns.

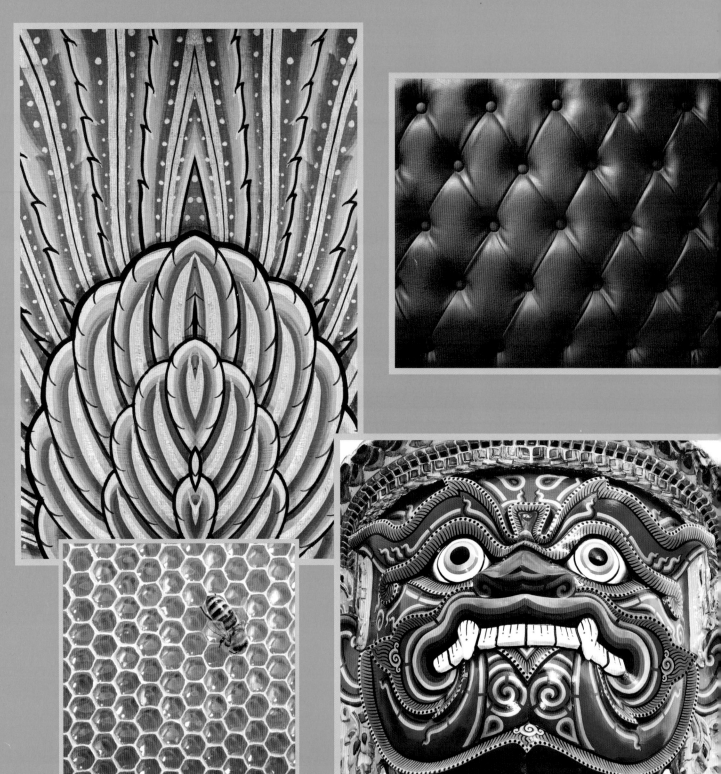

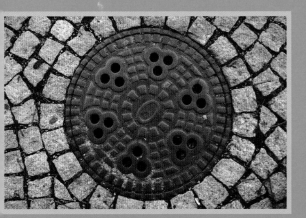

MathSpeak

Mathematicians use special words to describe patterns. Check out these speech balloons if you want to talk MathSpeak, too.

4

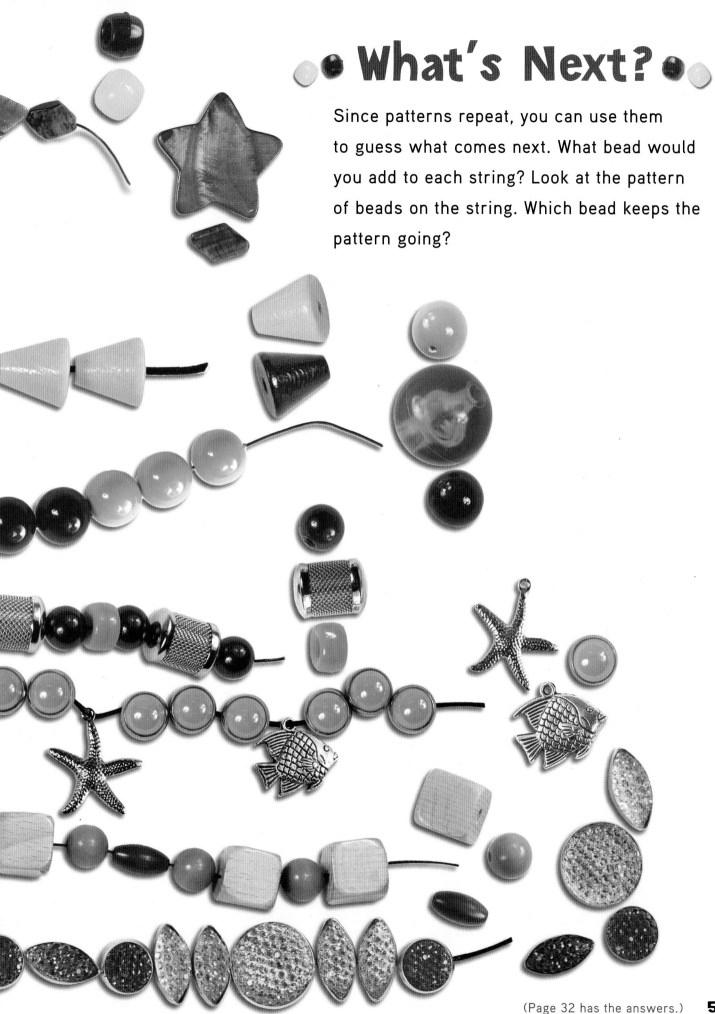

What's Next?

Since patterns repeat, you can use them to guess what comes next. What bead would you add to each string? Look at the pattern of beads on the string. Which bead keeps the pattern going?

(Page 32 has the answers.) **5**

You can make patterns by moving shapes, too. Sliding a shape is the easiest way to make a pattern. You can slide this seal in any direction. It might slide left, right, up, down, or diagonally.

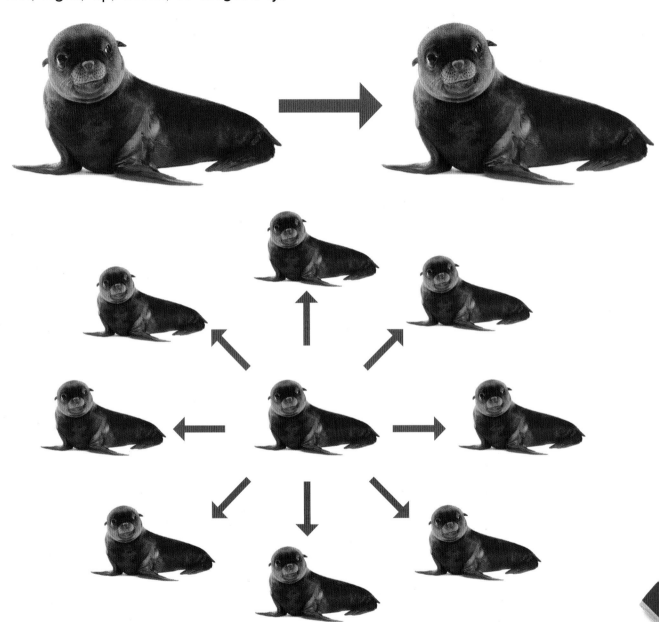

MathSpeak

SLIDE = TRANSLATION

The math word for *slide* is *translation*. That doesn't mean naming a shape in another language. In math, a **translation** is a move from one place to another.

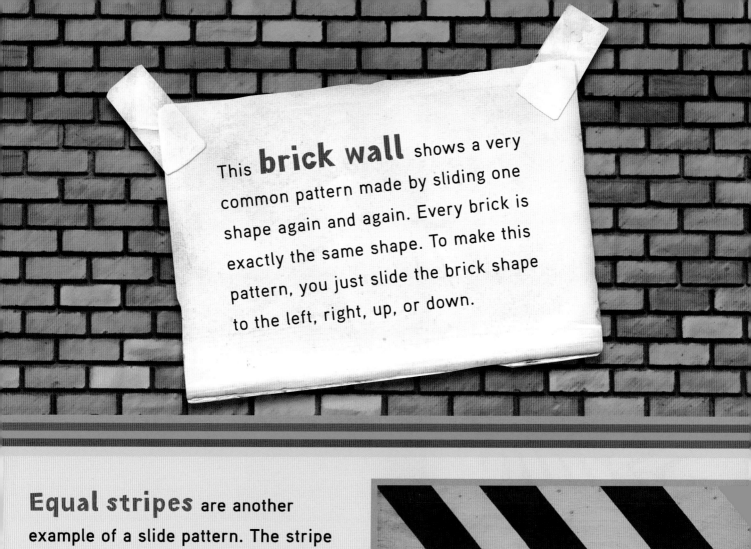

This **brick wall** shows a very common pattern made by sliding one shape again and again. Every brick is exactly the same shape. To make this pattern, you just slide the brick shape to the left, right, up, or down.

Equal stripes are another example of a slide pattern. The stripe moves, or slides, in one direction.

Fabrics can show fabulous patterns. This Indian cloth shows a **block print**. First, an artist carved the pattern into a wooden block. Then the artist rolled ink on the block and stamped the fabric again and again.

Another artist used a **stencil** to paint this temple wall in Laos. To make the stencil, the artist cut a pattern out of a thin sheet of paper or other material. Then the painter placed the stencil on the wall and painted the part of the wall that showed through the holes. Finally the painter slid the stencil over and repeated.

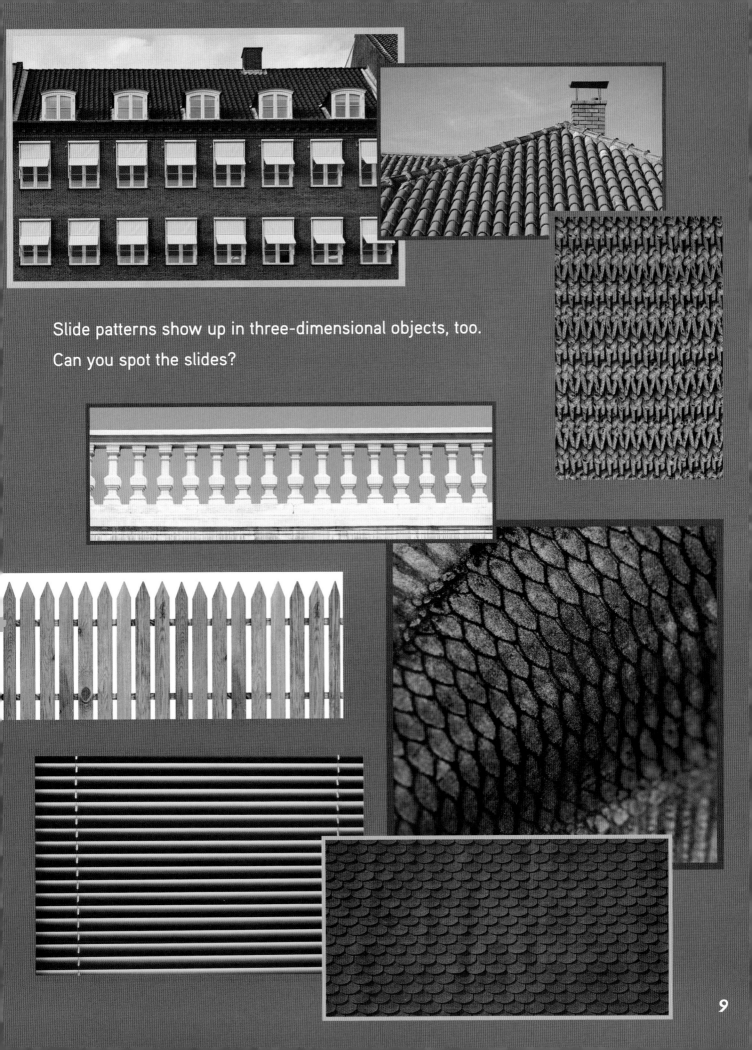

Slide patterns show up in three-dimensional objects, too.
Can you spot the slides?

Turn It Around

You can also make a pattern by turning a shape. You can turn this turtle just a little bit, a whole lot, or anything in between. You can also turn it clockwise or counterclockwise.

Many patterns turn shapes upside down. This **cloak** made in Peru about two thousand years ago shows a pattern made by turning a mythological creature.

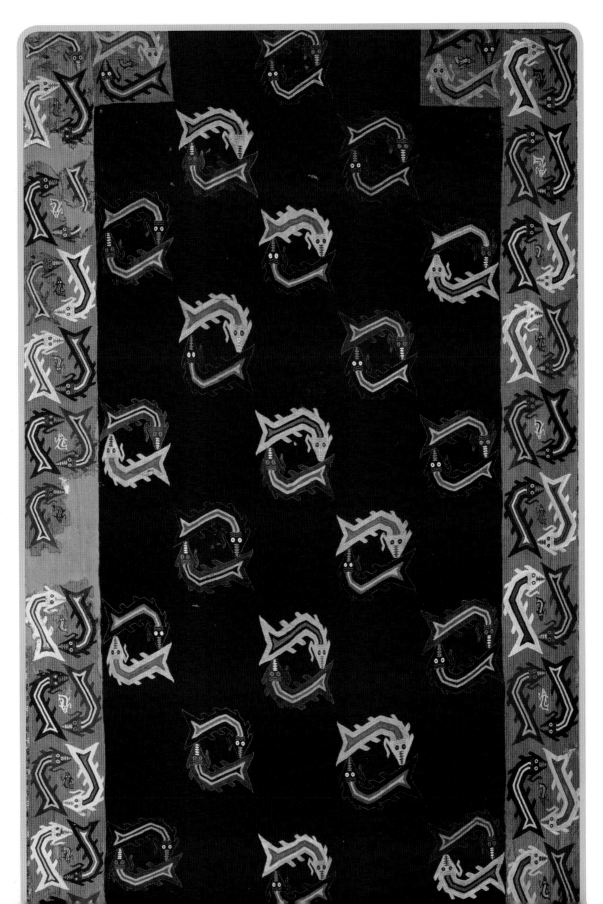

Can you spot some upside-down turns in this **mud cloth** from Africa? Artists in Mali make these designs by leaving special mud on the fabric for a long time—up to a year! When the time's up, they wash off the mud. Dyes from the mud leave patterns on the cloth.

MathSpeak

UPSIDE DOWN = 180-DEGREE TURN

Degrees are a way to measure how much you turn a shape. There are 360 degrees in a circle. When you turn a shape upside down, you turn it 180 degrees.

You'll often find turn patterns on round things, such as plates, baskets, tires, and saw blades.

13

Flipping Out

Another way to make a pattern is to flip a shape over. Notice that the flamingo is facing the other way when you flip it over. That's how you can tell that this is a flip, not a turn.

To think about flips, imagine folding. If you fold this page on the dotted line, these two shapes will match up.

MathSpeak

FLIP = REFLECTION

A **reflection** flips a shape across a line called the **line of reflection**.

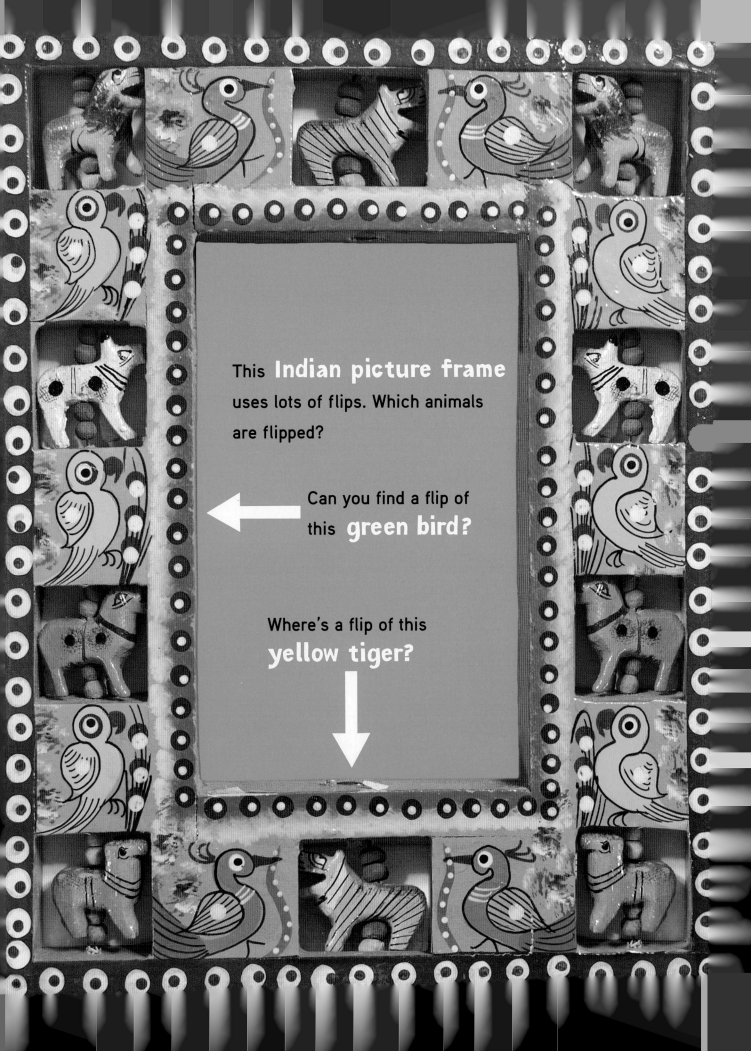

This **Indian picture frame** uses lots of flips. Which animals are flipped?

Can you find a flip of this **green bird?**

Where's a flip of this **yellow tiger?**

Flip patterns show up in fancy designs, such as lace and silk fabric.

But you'll also find them on everyday things, such as tire treads, boxing gloves, mittens, and the bottoms of your shoes.

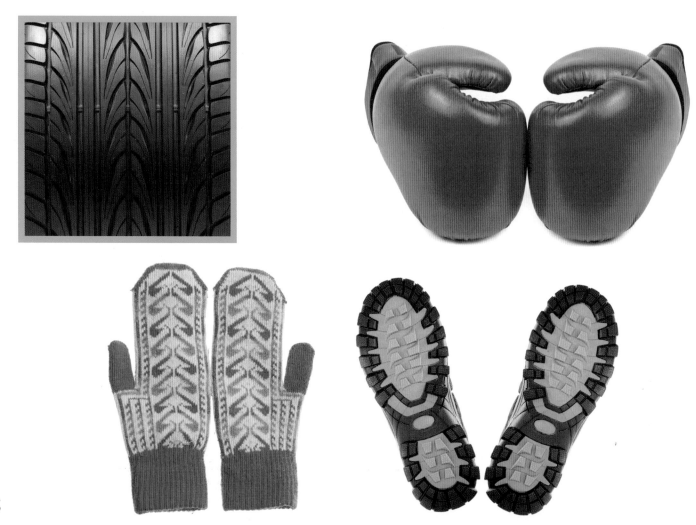

A **kaleidoscope** uses mirrors to make flip patterns. You get beautiful pictures when you see the objects and their flipped images at the same time. These days you don't even need a kaleidoscope to make these patterns. You can use a computer. Notice how a triangle from this bird photo can be flipped again and again to make a kaleidoscope picture.

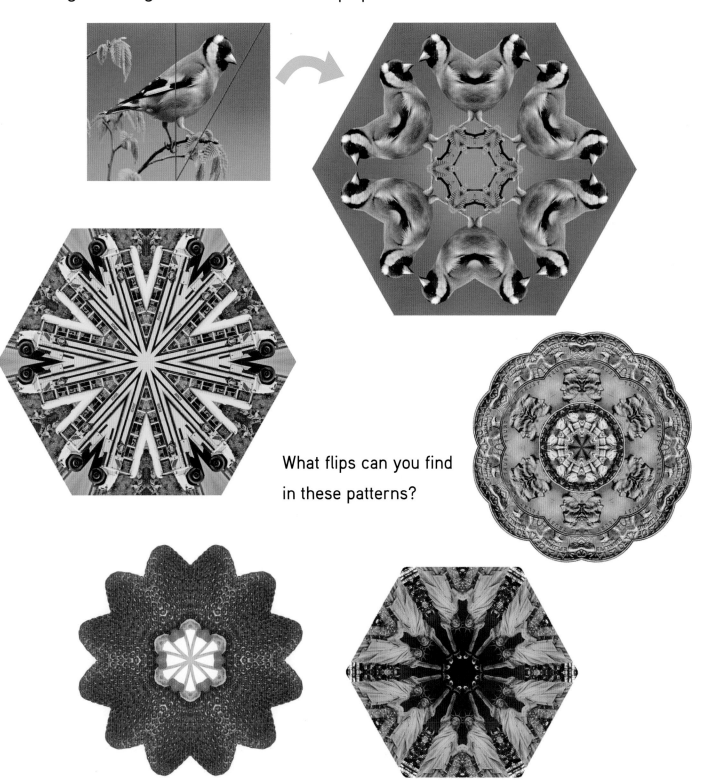

What flips can you find
in these patterns?

 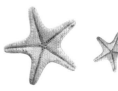

Follow the Fold

Sometimes, you'll spot flips inside shapes, too. If you think of folding this picture of a frog down the middle, the two sides match exactly.

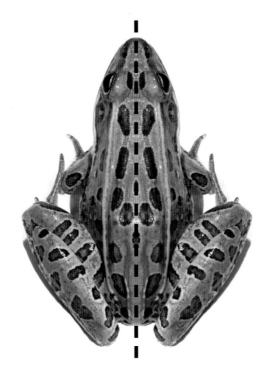

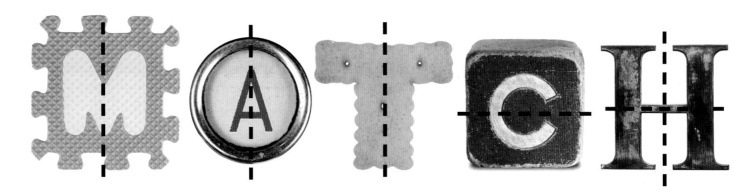

MathSpeak

EQUAL SIDES = SYMMETRY

A shape has **symmetry** if you could fold it so that two sides match. The line you fold along is the **line of symmetry**. Shapes can have more than one line of symmetry.

You can see this kind of pattern in objects people make as well as in nature. All these pictures can be folded in at least one way to get equal halves. Can you figure out where the fold lines are?

(You'll find answers on page 32.) **19**

One Size Doesn't Fit All

Sometimes, a pattern uses the same shape in different sizes.
You can make this sparrow bigger or smaller.

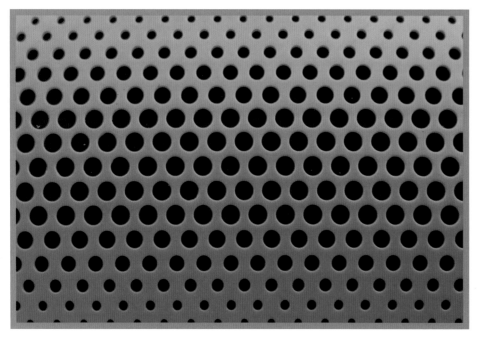

This pattern shows circles cut out of metal. All the circles are the same shape, but there are many different sizes.

MathSpeak

CHANGING SIZES = SCALING

Scaling is changing the size of a shape. If you make the shape bigger, you **increase** the scale. If you make it smaller, you **decrease** the scale.

This **tile mosaic** from the Apollo Temple in Corinth, Greece, uses triangles that get smaller and smaller toward the center of the design.

The **Pantheon dome** is in Rome, Italy. When you look up from the center of this temple, you see a circle of sky surrounded by squares of many different sizes.

Squish It! Stretch It!

Some patterns stretch and squish shapes to change them.

This squirrel squishes.

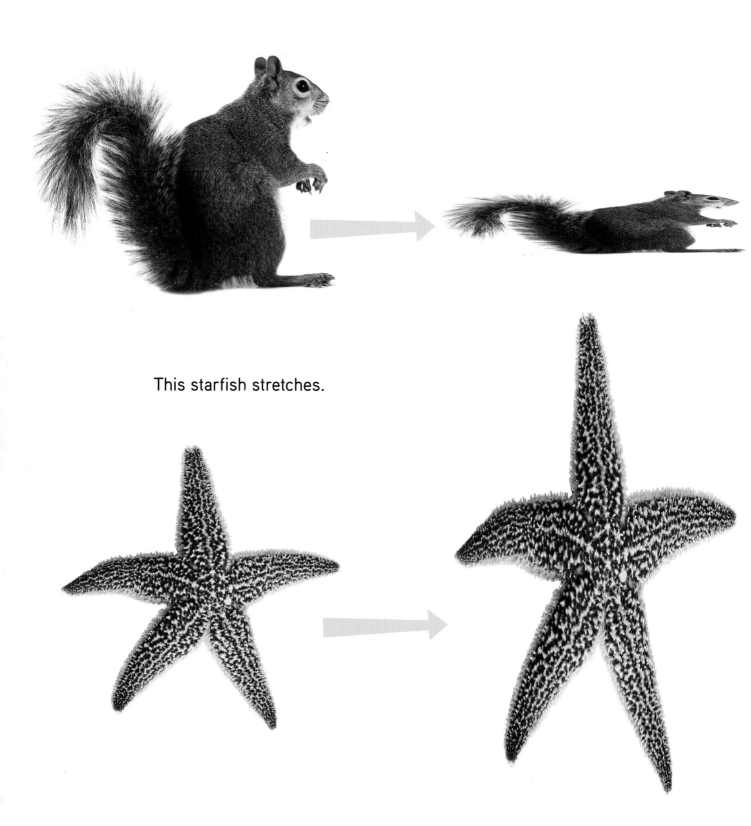

This starfish stretches.

This **Mexican blanket** uses a stripe pattern, but instead of equal stripes, it stretches some stripes so they are wider, and squishes others so they are narrower.

In this **rug,** the shapes get smaller as they move toward the center, but that's not all. They get narrower, too. In order for the pattern to fit, the designer had to squish the shapes.

Color Counts

Of course, shapes aren't the only important thing when you're looking at patterns. Color counts for a lot, too.

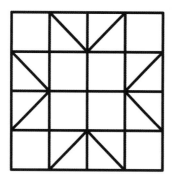

Here's a classic quilt pattern sometimes called **Sawtooth Star.** It's made by sewing together triangles and squares.

Depending on what colors you use, the same pattern can look very different. Notice how this simple pattern changes when you rearrange just three colors.

The differences pop out even more when
you sew four Sawtooth Star blocks together.

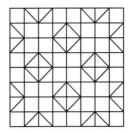

Imagine how many other patterns are possible if you add more colors!

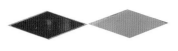 # Erase the Space

Many patterns have empty space between shapes that slide, turn, or flip. A tile pattern covers a flat area with no space between the tiles. Some shapes, such as squares and rectangles, are perfect for making tile patterns. Other shapes, such as circles, don't form tile patterns because, even when you push them right next to each other, there's always some space in between.

This **checkerboard** shows a common tile pattern. The wood and black squares cover the board completely.

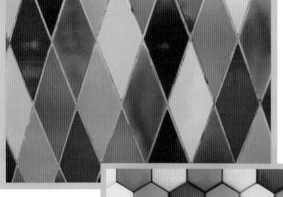

Diamonds and triangles can cover a space without leaving any gaps, too. So can six-sided shapes called hexagons.

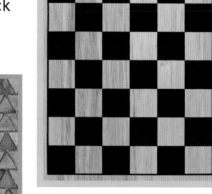

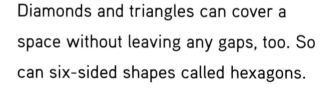

Houndstooth fabric uses a tile pattern, too. Apparently someone who named this pattern thought it looked like a dog's back teeth.

Some tile patterns combine more than one shape. This **patio** combines squares and octagons (shapes with eight sides).

The **Alhambra** is a palace in Granada, Spain. Here are just a few of the tile shapes and patterns that decorate its walls.

Mix and Match

So do you see a pattern here? You can see a lot of them now. Slides, turns, flips, symmetry, changing sizes, and tiling—this mosaic pattern uses all of them! Patterns can combine different ways of changing shapes to create an amazing variety of effects. What changes can you spot?

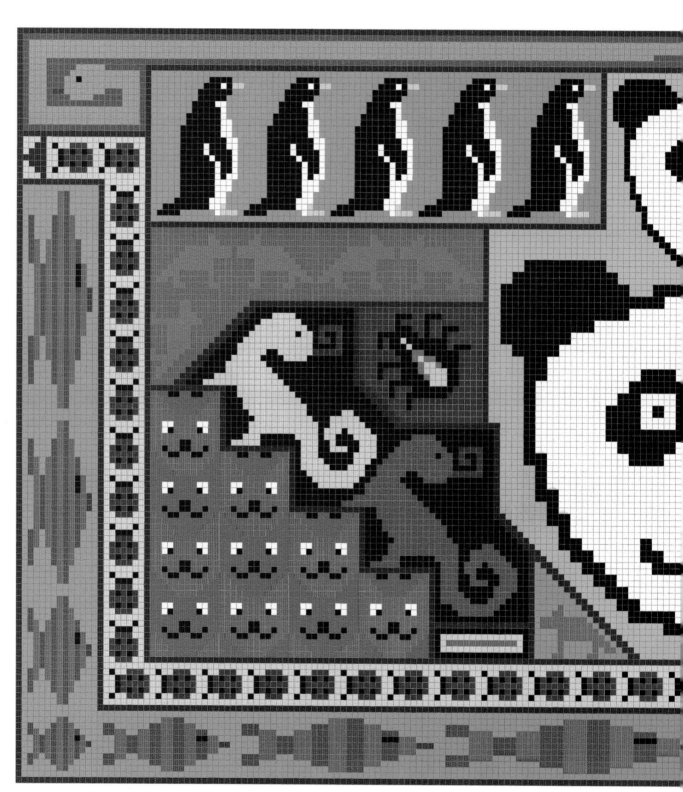

Any time you change a shape, you **transform** it. Translation, rotation, reflection, and scaling are different kinds of **transformations**.

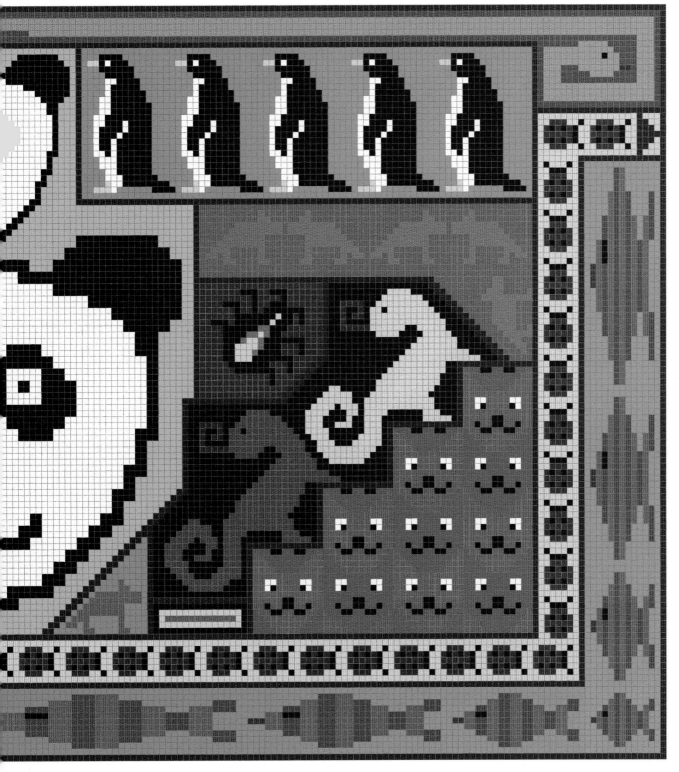

29

 # Repeat After Me

Some ideas for creating your own patterns

BUILDING BLOCKS

Next time you pull out your plastic blocks, make a pattern. You might build a pattern that repeats again and again, or one that grows. When you're done building, pass your structure to a friend. Can your friend find and continue your pattern?

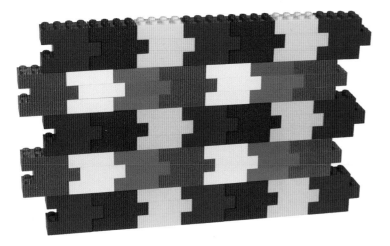

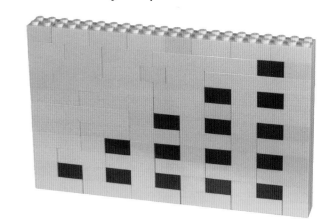

STAMPS

Stamps are great for making patterns with slides and turns. You can use rubber stamps and ink pads or carve your own shapes out of a potato and apply poster paint. Your patterns can decorate book covers, wrapping paper, posters, notebooks, and T-shirts.

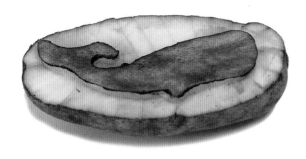

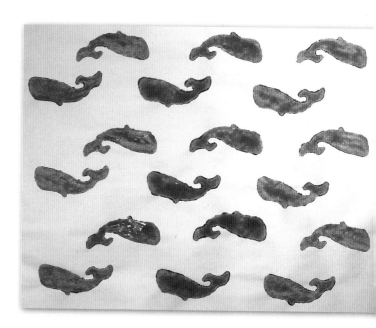

PAPER CUTOUTS

Scissors and construction paper are all you need to make some terrific flip patterns. Make paper doll chains by folding a sheet in half and then in half again. Draw the shape you want to cut out. Be sure that some of the shape goes over the folded edges so your paper dolls will hold together when you cut them out. Your chains can be people, animals like these squirrels, or any other shape you want.

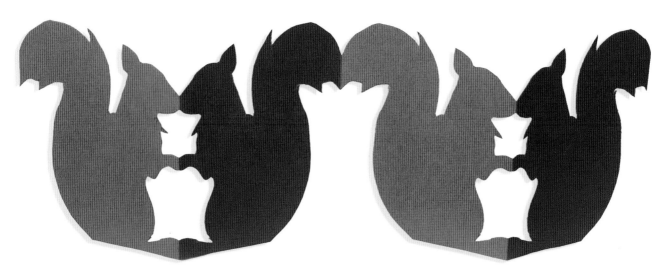

You get another kind of flip pattern when you fold a square in half along the diagonal and then fold that triangle in half twice more. This is how you get snowflakes or rings of flipping shapes, like these snakes.

ANSWER KEY

What's Next?

Since patterns repeat, you can use them to guess what comes next. What bead would you add to each string? Look at the pattern of beads on the string. Which bead keeps the pattern going?

5

You can see this kind of pattern in objects people make as well as in nature. All these pictures can be folded in at least one way to get equal halves. Can you figure out where the fold lines are?

19

Thanks to Lisa Schmidt of Good Press Ceramics for the wonderful tessellating walrus tile.

Henry Holt and Company, LLC, *Publishers since 1866*
175 Fifth Avenue, New York, New York 10010
mackids.com

Henry Holt® is a registered trademark of Henry Holt and Company, LLC.

All photographs by Bruce Goldstone, except on the following pages: 2, 3, 6–9, 13–14, 16–23, 26–27, © Shutterstock; 11 (Peruvian cloth), Nasca [*Mantle*, 0–100 c.e., cotton, camelid fiber, textile: 118⅛ x 63¾ in. (300 x 162 cm), Brooklyn Museum—Alfred W. Jenkins Fund, 34.1560]; 26 (walrus tile), © Lisa Schmidt/Good Press Ceramics.

Library of Congress Cataloging-in-Publication Data
Goldstone, Bruce.
I see a pattern here / Bruce Goldstone.
pages   cm
Audience: Age 7–10.
ISBN 978-0-8050-9209-7 (hardback)
1. Pattern perception—Juvenile literature. I. Title.
BF294.G65 2015   152.14'23—dc23   2014028433

Henry Holt books may be purchased for business or promotional use. For information on bulk purchases, please contact Macmillan Corporate and Premium Sales Department at (800) 221-7945 x5442 or by e-mail at specialmarkets@macmillan.com.

First Edition—2015 / Designed by April Ward and Anna Booth
Printed in China by Toppan Leefung Printing Ltd., Dongguan City, Guangdong Province

1 3 5 7 9 10 8 6 4 2